A New True Book

TROPICAL RAIN FORESTS

By Emilie U. Lepthien

EIC
WSU Vancouver Library

CHILDRENS PRESS®
CHICAGO

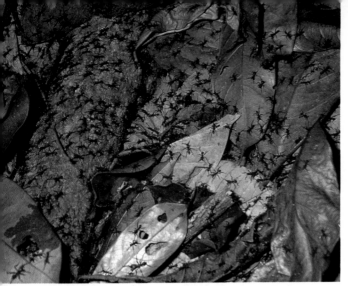

No one knows how many kinds of
rain forest plants and insects are yet
to be discovered and named
by scientists.

Project Editor: Fran Dyra
Design: Margrit Fiddle

Library of Congress Cataloging-in-Publication Data

Lepthien, Emilie U. (Emilie Utteg)
    Tropical rain forests / by Emilie U. Lepthien.
        p.   cm. — (A New true book)
    Includes index.
    Summary: Describes the structure of a rain forest,
typical plant and animal life, climate, and the need for
conservation.
    ISBN 0-516-01198-7
    1. Rain forest ecology—Juvenile literature.
2. Rain forests—Juvenile literature. 3. Ecology.
[1. Rain forests. 2. Rain forest ecology.]
I. Title.
QH541.5.R27L455   1993
574.5'2642'0913—dc20   93-3408
                                              CIP
                                               AC

PHOTO CREDITS

AP/Wide World Photos—Cover Inset, 28

© Reinhard Brucker—34 (center & right)

Tom Dunnington—maps 4, 8

GeoIMAGERY—© Jan & Al Jorolan, 16 (left);
© Hermine Dreyfuss, 19 (right)

H. Armstrong Roberts—25 (top); © E.R.
Degginger, Cover, 20 (left)

Odyssey/Frerck/Chicago—© Robert Frerck, 13

Chip and Rosa Maria de la Cueva Peterson—12

Photri—© M. Bruce, 18 (left)

Root Resources—© Thomas C. Boyden, 2, 17
(right), 27, 32, 37; © Anthony Mercieca, 43 (left)

© James P. Rowan—41

Tom Stack & Associates—© Chip & Jill
Isenhart, 4, 22; © D. G. Barker, 16 (right); © Jack
Swenson, 17 (left); © Kevin Schafer, 38

Tony Stone Images—36, © Nigel Dickinson, 7,
34 (left); © David Austen, 9, 45; © Robert Frerck,
11; © Norbert Wu, 14 (bottom); © David Hiser,
30; © G. Brad Lewis, 44

SuperStock International, Inc.—© M. Sutton, 14
(top); © S. Gould, 23 (left); © H. Kanus, 23
(right); © E. Manewal, 25 (bottom); © G.
Seymour, 33; © A. Mercieca, 43 (right)

Valan—© Karl Weidmann, 18 (right); © Jeff
Foott, 19 (left); © Stephen J. Krasemann, 20
(right), 40; © John Cancalosi, 31

Cover: Monteverde Rain Forest, Costa Rica

Cover Inset: Slash and burn, Porto Velho, Brazil

TABLE OF CONTENTS

What Is a Tropical Rain
    Forest?...5

The Five Layers of a Tropical Rain
    Forest...8

Rain Forest Habitats...15

Rain Forest Soil...21

Who Lives in Rain Forests?...22

The Disappearing Rain Forest..26

Slash and Burn...30

Rain Forest Treasures...33

Rain Forests and World
    Climates...36

Protecting the Rain Forests...39

Debt-for-Nature Swaps...42

We Can Help...43

Words You Should Know...46

Index...48

Above: A tropical rain forest in Costa Rica.   Below: The world's most important rain forests lie in the area between the Tropic of Cancer and the Tropic of Capricorn.

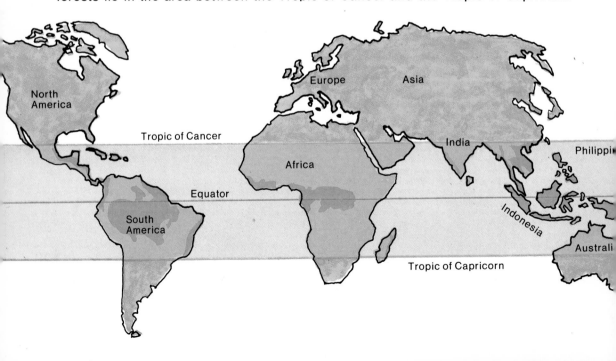

WHAT IS A TROPICAL RAIN FOREST?

Tropical rain forests are the world's richest forests. They cover only seven percent of the Earth's land. Yet, more than half of the world's plant and animal species live in tropical rain forests.

The most important rain forests are near the equator. They lie in the tropics–the area between the Tropic of Cancer and the Tropic of Capricorn.

Tropical rain forests grow in Central America, South America, Africa, India and Sri Lanka, Southeast Asia, and on islands in the Pacific Ocean.

Almost 50 percent of the world's tropical rain forests are in Brazil, Zaire, and Indonesia.

Tropical rain forests are warm, wet, and green all year. The temperature rarely goes above 93°F (34°C) or drops below 68°F (20°C).

Mist rises from a humid rain forest in Malaysia.

The sun shines almost every day. But the forest's warm, humid air holds so much moisture that it also rains almost every day. At least 80 inches (203 centimeters) of rain falls each year.

THE FIVE LAYERS OF A TROPICAL RAIN FOREST

If you could cut through a rain forest like a cake, you would find five layers. From top to bottom, these layers are:

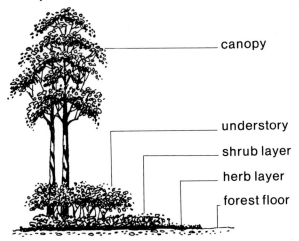

canopy

understory

shrub layer

herb layer

forest floor

The canopy is made up of tall trees that tower 75 to 150 feet (23 to 45 meters) above the forest floor.

A hut in a forest clearing in New Guinea. People who live in rain forests use the materials of the forest to build homes.

The tops of the tallest trees rise above the canopy. These tall trees, called emergents, may grow 200 feet (61 meters) high.

The overlapping branches of the canopy allow very little sunlight and rain to reach the forest floor.

The understory is made up of smaller trees. They may reach only 12 feet (4 meters) in height. The air in the understory is very humid. The temperature is high— about 90°F (32°C).

The shrub layer consists of woody plants that grow up to 6 feet (2 meters) high And herb layer has small green plants.

Opposite page: Ferns and grasses grow in the shrub layer of a tropical rain forest.

Trail through a rain forest in Panama

The forest floor is covered
with a thin layer of fallen
leaves. Fungi and insects
thrive in the shallow soil and
leaf litter.

Because so little rain and

sunlight reach the forest

floor, not many plants grow there. So it is often easy to walk through a rain forest.

Jungle, or dense vegetation, is found in places where more sunlight reaches the ground.

Jungle growth along a riverbank in southern Mexico

Epiphytes grow on forest
trees (above). They help trees
grow by increasing the humidity.
Then the trees can absorb nitrogen
from the air more easily.
Lianas (left) twine around the
trunks of rain forest trees.

RAIN FOREST HABITATS

Each layer of the rain forest provides a special home for plants and animals.

Climbing plants and thick vines called lianas grow from the forest floor. They twine around the trunks and branches of trees. These plants and vines connect the different layers of the rain forest.

Epiphytes are air plants. They are found in every layer. Epiphytes grow on other plants and get their

Grass orchids (left) and a rain forest frog (right).
The frog's bright colors warn that it is poisonous.

food and moisture from the
air. Orchids are epiphytes.
There are over two thousand
kinds of orchids in rain forests.
Frogs, ants, and other
small animals hide among

16

the epiphytes and use them for nesting.

Monkeys, bats, and birds live in the canopy and understory. They feed on fruits, insects, and leaves.

In South America, slow-moving sloths hang high in

White-faced monkeys (left) live in Costa Rica. The cacique bird (below) weaves a pouchlike nest of grasses.

Sloths (left) sleep hanging upside down from tree branches. Ocelots (right) look like small leopards.

the trees. In Central and South America, jaguars and ocelots hide in the branches of trees to wait for their prey. They drop down onto the backs of deer and tapirs. African civets hunt in the same way.

In Africa, giant forest hogs roam the forest floor. They feed on leaves and small plant shoots. Africa's lowland gorillas spend time on the forest floor and sometimes sleep in the understory.

Giant forest hog (left) and lowland gorilla (below)

Lizards (left) and agouti (right) live on the forest floor.

Rats, lizards, frogs, and
the capybara and agouti of
Central and South America
are ground dwellers. In
Southeast Asia, tapirs feed
on twigs, fruits, and grasses.

RAIN FOREST SOIL

Tropical rain forests have a thin layer of soil that is very poor in minerals. Most of the forest's minerals and other nutrients are found in its plants and animals. When these plants and animals die, they rot quickly. In this way, their nutrients are recycled in a short time.

The roots of the trees and plants lie near the surface, where they can use these nutrients.

ENVIRONMENTAL INFORMATION CENTER
1200 Ft. Vancouver Way • P. O. Box 8900
Vancouver, Wa 98668   (206) 699-3325

WHO LIVES
IN RAIN FORESTS?

People have lived in rain forests for thousands of years. They use forest products for food, clothing, and shelter. They have also found hundreds of plants that can be used as natural medicines.

Medicines from the local rain forest are sold in Costa Rica.

Rain forest peoples: The Choco of Panama (left) and the Yanomami of Venezuela (right). Yanomami hunters use darts from long blowguns to kill small animals.

Today, there may be as many as 200 million people living in the world's rain forests. Some of these people are hunters and gatherers.

In the Amazon rain forest, people have been farmers for hundreds of years. They cut

23

down small patches of forest and burn the trees. The ashes provide food for the crops the farmers plant.

Quick-growing sweet potatoes and other crops are planted. After a few years, the farmers plant trees on that land and clear another small plot for raising vegetables. Over time, the first plot becomes rain forest again.

Rain forest farmers plant small patches of corn, squash, beans, tomatoes, rice, and sugarcane. Their wood and grass houses (below) are built in forest clearings.

THE DISAPPEARING RAIN FOREST

Rain forests once covered an area almost twice as large as the continental United States. Today only about half of that forested land remains. And every year more and more forested land is lost.

Within one hundred years, the world's rain forests may be completely destroyed.

This deforestation is taking place in at least forty-five countries around the

Sawmill along the Amazon River. Tropical hardwoods are sold to Japan, the United States, and European countries.

equator. Large areas are being opened up for logging. Valuable tropical hardwoods, teak, mahogany, rosewood, balsa, sandalwood, and purple heartwood are cut down and sold to other countries.

There may be up to one hundred species of trees in 1 acre (0.4 hectare) of rain forest. And in order to cut down a few valuable trees, loggers often destroy an entire forest area.

Malaysia, the Philippines, Indonesia, Ivory Coast, and

When roads are cut through the rain forest, many plants and animals may be destroyed. But the people of tropical countries claim that roads are needed for economic development.

Gabon account for most of these exports. Today, thirty countries sell tropical hardwoods. But these hardwood forests are disappearing rapidly. In twenty years there may be only ten countries with enough wood to export.

Over half of the wood taken from rain forests is used in the country where it grows. Some is used for fuel and fence posts. Wood is also made into charcoal and used in brick factories, iron smelters, and cement plants.

Settlers clear the tropical rain forest for farms. But the forest soil is not rich enough for large-scale farming, and the farms are soon abandoned.

SLASH AND BURN

Some forest areas have been opened up to provide land for new settlers. Roads are built and land is given to poor farmers. These settlers use a method called slash-and-burn farming.

First they cut down all the trees and other plants and burn them. Then the farmers plant their crops among the ashes.

At first, the crops do well because some nutrients from the burned plants are released into the soil. But

Planting corn among the ashes. In this plot, the fires have not burned away all the tree branches.

Cattle ranchers may take over abandoned farms for a while. But in a few years, the soil will not grow enough to feed the cattle.

these new farmers do not move on to let the soil recover, as the older farmers did.

After a few years, their crops do poorly because the soil is too shallow and lacking in nutrients. The soil is ruined, and these

farms are soon abandoned.

Harvesting cocoa in Zaire, Africa

RAIN FOREST TREASURES

As each acre of rain forest is destroyed, the world loses much more than trees.

Cocoa, rubber, bananas, and pineapples are among the many crops that first grew in rain forests. Many

33

A woman picks herbs for medicine in Southeast Asia (left). Vanilla (center) and nutmeg (right) are among our favorite flavors. Did you know that they come from rain forests?

different spices, nuts, fruits, oils, resins, and fibers also come from rain forests.

And the rain forest is nature's drugstore. The products of the rain forest include medicines that treat glaucoma, malaria, and Parkinson's disease. And drugs that lower blood pressure, quiet irregular heartbeat, and stop the growth of cancer cells also come from rain forests.

When the trees and other plants are destroyed, the soil of the forest floor is easily blown or washed away. Many species of plants and animals lose their habitats. Many become extinct before they can even be studied by scientists. And the chance to find cures for diseases may be lost forever.

RAIN FORESTS
AND WORLD CLIMATES

The world's climates will be changed if the rain forests disappear. More than half of the rainfall in the tropical forests is produced by the trees and plants themselves. But deforested

This hot and dry land was cleared for cattle ranching. The region was once covered with lush, cool rain forest.

lands reflect sunlight back into space. Wind currents and rainfall far from the tropics will be changed.

The burning of tropical rain forests releases tons of carbon dioxide into the atmosphere. Increased carbon dioxide may be one cause of "global warming" that could affect our environment.

PROTECTING THE RAIN FORESTS

Many organizations are working to protect the rain forests. The Smithsonian Institution, World Wildlife Fund, Nature Conservancy, and the governments of many nations are engaged in the effort.

National parks have been developed in many rain forest areas. Costa Rica, Belize, Peru, Brazil, Mexico,

Opposite page: Each time even a small area of rain forest is destroyed, several species of plants and animals are lost forever.

Rain forest along a creek in Cuyabeno Reserve, Ecuador

Ecuador, Indonesia, the Philippines, Bolivia, Madagascar, and Zambia have established national parks and reserves to protect their rain forests.

41

DEBT-FOR-NATURE SWAPS

Many countries with rain forests owe millions of dollars to banks in other countries. Conservation groups may pay part of a nation's debt if the country uses the money it saves for conservation. Only countries with strong conservation programs are accepted in debt-for-nature swaps.

WE CAN HELP

The destruction of tropical rain forests affects us all. How can we help?

Many birds, plants, and animals are taken illegally from rain forests. We should never buy these birds, plants, or animals.

Colorful birds (left) and iguanas (below) are taken illegally from rain forests and sold as pets.

A crowd gathers in Hawaii to protest the destruction of rain forests.

We can support conservation groups. We can learn more. We can help others understand how important rain forests are to the whole world. We can recycle waste materials. And each of us can plant a tree.

WORDS YOU SHOULD KNOW

agouti (uh • GOO • tee) — a rodent about the size of a rabbit

balsa (BAWL • sa) — a very lightweight wood

canopy (KAN • uh • pee) — the top layer of a rain forest, where the branches form a covering of leaves

capybara (KAP • ee • BAH • rah) — an animal that looks like a small pig

carbon dioxide (KAR • bun dye • OX • ide) — a gas in the air that is made up of carbon and oxygen

charcoal (CHAR • kole) — partially burned wood that is used as fuel

civet (SIV • it) — a catlike animal with spotted fur

conservation (kahn • zer • VAY • shun) — the saving of the Earth's forests, minerals, and other resources

debt (DET) — an amount of money that is owed to a bank or other lender

deforestation (dee • for • ess • TAY • shun) — the removal of all trees and other plants in a forest area

emergents (ee • MER • jents) — very tall trees whose tops reach above the rain forest canopy

epiphytes (EH • pih • fytes) — plants that rest on other plants for support and get their food and water from the air

equator (ih • KWAY • ter) — an imaginary line around the Earth, equally distant from the North and South poles

export (EX • port) — to send products out of one country for sale in another country

extinct (ex • TINKT) — no longer living

fibers (FYE • berz) — threadlike plant parts or animal hairs used for making cloth or rope

fungi (FUNG • eye) — plants, such as mushrooms, that have no flowers, leaves, or green color

glaucoma (glaw • KOH • ma) — a disease of the eyes

habitat (HAB • ih • tat) — home; the place where an animal usually lives

hardwood (HARD • wood) — valuable wood that is used for furniture and building

herb (ERB) — a plant with a soft green stem

humid (HYOO • mid) — damp; moist

jaguar (JAG • wahr) — a large, spotted cat that lives in Central and South America

lianas (lee • AN • ahz) — vines with thick, woody stems that twine around trees

mahogany (muh • HAWG • uh • nee) — a heavy, dark wood that is used for fine furniture

malaria (muh • LAIR • ee • uh) — a disease that causes chills and fever

nutrients (NOO • tree • ents) — minerals and other substances in food or soil that are needed for good health by plants and animals

ocelot (AH • sih • lot) — a medium-sized spotted cat of Central and South America

orchid (OR • kid) — a plant that lives on other plants and that has large, showy flowers

Parkinson's disease (PAR • kin • sunz dih • ZEEZ) — a disease of the nervous system

resin (REH • zin) — a sticky substance that comes from trees or plants, used in varnishes or medicines

sloth (SLAWTH) — a slow-moving animal with long, coarse fur that lives in trees

smelter (SMEL • ter) — a place where mineral ores are melted to separate the metals

species (SPEE • ceez) — a group of related plants or animals that are able to interbreed

tapir (TAY • per) — a large, piglike animal

teak (TEEK) — a heavy, durable wood used for furniture and shipbuilding

INDEX

Africa, 6, 18, 19
Amazon rain forest, 23-24
animals, 5, 15, 16, 17, 18, 19, 20, 21, 35, 43
ashes, 24, 32
balsa, 27
bananas, 24, 33
Belize, 39
birds, 17, 43
Bolivia, 41
Brazil, 6, 39
brick factories, 29
cancer, 35
canopy, 8, 9, 10, 17
carbon dioxide, 37
cement plants, 29
Central America, 6, 18, 20
charcoal, 29
climates, 36
cocoa, 33
conservation groups, 39, 42, 44
Costa Rica, 39
crops, 24, 31, 32, 33
debt-for-nature swaps, 42
deforestation, 26, 36-37
Ecuador, 41
ephiphytes, 15, 16, 17
equator, 5, 27
farmers, 23-24, 30-32

forest floor. 8, 10, 12, 15, 19, 35
frogs, 16, 20
fruits, 17, 20, 34
fungi, 12
Gabon, 29
global warming, 37
hardwoods, 27, 29
herb layer, 8, 10
humidity, 7, 10
India, 6
Indonesia, 6, 28, 41
insects, 12, 17
iron smelters, 29
Ivory Coast, 28
jungle, 13
lianas, 15
logging, 27, 28
Madagascar, 41
mahogany, 27
Malaysia, 28
medicines, 22, 34
Mexico, 39
national parks, 39, 41
Nature Conservancy, 39
nutrients, 21, 24, 31, 32
nuts, 34
oils, 34
orchids, 16
Pacific Ocean, 6

people of rain forests, 22, 23
Peru, 39
Philippines, the, 28, 41
pineapples, 33
plants, 5, 10, 12, 15, 19, 21, 22, 31, 35, 36, 43
purple heartwood, 27
rain, 7, 10, 12, 36, 37
rosewood, 27
rubber, 33
sandalwood, 27
shrub layer, 8, 10
Smithsonian Institution, 39
soil, 12, 21, 24, 31, 32, 35
South America, 6, 17, 18, 20
Southeast Asia, 6, 20
spices, 34
Sri Lanka, 6
sunlight, 6, 10, 12, 13, 37
sweet potatoes, 24
tapirs, 18, 20
teak, 27
temperatures, 6, 10
Tropic of Cancer, 4, 5
Tropic of Capricorn, 4, 5
tropics, 5, 37
understory, 8, 10, 17, 19
wind currents, 37
World Wildlife Fund, 39
Zaire, 6
Zambia, 41

About the Author

Emilie U. Lepthien received her BA and MS degrees and certificate in school administration from Northwestern University. She taught upper-grade science and social studies, wrote and narrated science programs for the Chicago Public Schools' station WBEZ, and was principal in Chicago, Illinois, for twenty years. She received the American Educator's Medal from Freedoms Foundation.

She is a member of Delta Kappa Gamma Society International, Chicago Principals' Association, Illinois Women's Press Association, National Federation of Press Women, and AAUW.

She has written books in the Enchantment of the World, New True Books, and America the Beautiful series.